Writing to Describe

A Use-and-Keep Writing Portfolio

Level A

Author

Sally Speer Leber

Reviewers

Steve Graham
University of Maryland

Karen Harris
University of Maryland

The following teachers assisted in the development of the *Use-and-Keep Writing Portfolios* by field testing materials:

Susan Ford
St. Ann's School
Charlotte, North Carolina

Alice Kelly
Brookpark Memorial Elementary School
Brook Park, Ohio

Janice Weber
Stoker Elementary School
Kenosha, Wisconsin

Christine Geniusz
Brookpark Memorial Elementary School
Brook Park, Ohio

Janet Lewis
Southwest Elementary School
High Point, North Carolina

Donna Woosley
Forest Creek Elementary School
Round Rock, Texas

Beverly Hagenau
Prairie View Elementary School
Mukwonago, Wisconsin

Joan Motheral
Kirkmere Elementary School
Youngstown, Ohio

ISBN 0-88085-801-X

Zaner-Bloser, Inc., P.O. Box 16764, Columbus, Ohio 43216-6764, 1-800-421-3018

Printed in the United States of America

97 98 99 00 01 02 DKP 6 5 4 3 2

Writing to Describe

Table of Contents

Writing to Describe

This book will help you learn how to write a good descriptive essay. It will teach you the steps of the writing process. It will show you examples of descriptive writing.

When you have completed this book, it will help you with other writing assignments. Any time you need to write a description, you will be able to use it as a model. Keep your notes for this essay in the front pocket of this book. Put the other descriptive writing you do this year in the back pocket.

When Will You Write Descriptions?

You describe many things each day. You tell friends about television shows. You describe people, places, and things. Sometimes you write descriptions—in your journal, in letters, and in school. Study these examples of writing assignments.

Social Studies

- ✦ Create a travel ad describing a region of the United States or of the world that you have studied.
- ✦ In a letter to a pen pal, describe your community.

Science

- ✦ Carefully observe a seed sprouting and write a description of what you see each day.
- ✦ Create a book describing birds that visit a bird feeder at home or at school.

Math

- ✦ Take a walk outdoors. Look for patterns in things like leaves, butterflies, pine cones, spider webs, or sea shells. Sketch what you see and write descriptions later for a class book.

Language Arts

- ✦ Write an essay to describe ice cream for space aliens who have never tasted it.

Using the Writing Process to Write a Descriptive Essay

This *Use-and-Keep Writing Portfolio* will show you how to use the writing process to write a descriptive essay. The writing process has five steps. Notice that part of the process forms a loop. That's because writers often jump back and forth between the steps as they change their minds and think of new ideas.

The Steps of the Writing Process and You

As you become comfortable with the writing process, you can adjust the steps to fit the way you write.

You may not be sure what each of these words means. Here are the definitions:

PREWRITING means thinking and planning to help you get ready to write.

DRAFTING means writing your essay for the first time.

REVISING means making sure your writing makes sense and contains all the important information.

EDITING means correcting mistakes in spelling, punctuation, and grammar.

PUBLISHING means preparing your writing to be read by other people.

The writing process is not hard to learn. It will help you enjoy writing. It will also help you become a better writer. By the time you have worked through the writing process and completed this book, you'll be proud to share your work with others. You may find that you are eager to write more, too.

Writing Partners

As you use this book, you will work with a writing partner. You and your writing partner will help each other become better writers.

Each time you see this logo **discuss**, you will discuss your work with your writing partner. Whenever you see this logo **write**, you will write something in this book or on a separate sheet of paper.

Being a Good Writing Partner

Writing partners are nice to each other. They encourage each other, and they give good advice. Good writing partners think before they talk. They don't say things that might hurt their partner's feelings. They make suggestions to help improve their partner's writing.

Read the following comments. Would your feelings be hurt if someone said these things to you? Read the example, and then rewrite each comment. Try to say the same thing in a nicer, more helpful way.

write

Your spelling is awful. _Let's use the dictionary to check words that might be spelled wrong._

That's a dumb word to use. _____

_____

Your handwriting is a mess! _____

_____

That's a stupid idea! _____

_____

6

Agreeing on Goals and Rules

discuss   Writing partners must have the same goals. They also need to agree on rules before they begin to work together. Read the following agreement. Talk with your writing partner about rules that will help you work well together. When you agree on the rules, write them down.

write

Rules for Writing Partners

My name is _____

My writing partner is _____

We agree that our goal is to help each other become better writers. We agree to follow these rules when we work together:

_____

_____

_____

_____

_____

_____

_____

_____

Warming Up

> What do musicians do before a concert?
>
> What do athletes do before a game?
>
> What can writers do before they begin to write?
>
> **They warm up!**

Warm-ups get you in shape—to sing or play an instrument, to play a game, or to write. Warm-ups help you get ready. They help you get prepared.

You are going to write a descriptive essay. This means that you need to get prepared to give good descriptions. Playing a description game will help you and your partner warm up. You've probably played it before. It's called "What Am I?"

What Am I?

The goal of this game is to describe a person, place, or thing without using its name. If you give good descriptions, your partner will be able to come up with the right answer.

Rules of the Game:

1. Pick a person, a place, or a thing. Don't tell your partner who or what it is.

2. Begin your description with "I am" or "I have." (For example, if you were describing this book, you might say "I am made of paper" or "I have two pockets.")

3. Keep giving descriptive clues until your partner knows the answer. See how quickly you can help your partner come up with the right answer.

Using Descriptive Words

When you write to describe, you must use colorful and specific words. They will make your writing more interesting by creating vivid word pictures. Let's practice by reviewing nouns, adjectives, verbs, and adverbs.

Nouns
A noun names a person, place, or thing.

Here are some nouns:
sheepdog	robin	kickball
baseball	parrot	waterfall

Verbs
A verb shows action or being.

Here are some action verbs:
jumped	flew	bounced
chirped	danced	flowed

Adjectives
An adjective describes a noun by telling *which one? what kind of? how many?*

Here are some adjectives:
orange	new	giant
shaggy	seven	plump

Adverbs
An adverb describes a verb by telling *how? when? where? how much?*

Here are some adverbs:
up	loudly	excitedly
swiftly	yesterday	high

Study the examples below. Then fill in the blanks using words from the boxes above or your own colorful, descriptive words.

write

	Noun	More Descriptive Noun	Adjective and Noun
1.	dog	sheepdog	shaggy sheepdog
2.	bird		
3.	ball		
4.	water		

	Adjective and Noun	Action Verb	Adverb
1.	shaggy sheepdog	jumped	excitedly
2.			
3.			
4.			

Choosing Your Topic

You are going to write a descriptive essay. As in the game you just played, you will describe a person, a place, or a thing.

Good writers need good topics. You must select a topic that you already know well, one you don't have to research. You will enjoy writing more if you really like your topic. So let's think about your **favorite** people, **favorite** places, and **favorite** things.

write

Think about your favorite people, places, and things. Then write as many topic ideas as you can in the space below.

People

_____

_____

_____

_____

_____

Places

_____

_____

_____

_____

Things

_____

_____

_____

_____

Some topics are too broad. That means that there is too much to say about them. For example, you might want to describe Canada. But Canada is a big country. You couldn't possibly describe everything about Canada in one essay. The topic of Canada would be too broad. It would be better to choose one part of Canada to describe.

Perhaps you want to write about your collection of rocks. Instead of trying to describe the whole collection, you could focus on one special rock. It is important to keep the size of your topics in mind as you think about your choices.

discuss Share your list of possible topics (page 10) with your writing partner. Read each other's lists. Talk about each idea. Then discuss these questions:

✦ Are any of your topics too broad?

✦ Which topics would be the most fun to write about?

✦ Which topics would be easiest to describe?

✦ Who is going to read your description?

✦ Which topics would your readers enjoy the most?

Choose Your Topic

Look at your list of possible topics one more time. Think about the discussion you had with your writing partner. Record your choice below.

write

My topic is _____

Observing

You can learn a lot by observing. Taking a close look helps you see details. Details create good descriptions. Sometimes you can actually look at or watch a person, place, or thing. Other times, you can observe by recalling your memories. You can also observe by listening.

In this book, you will see the work of a student named Lee. Lee has the same assignment that you have. Lee really likes his grandpa's old car. He has decided to write his descriptive essay about the car.

To begin his observation, Lee drew a picture of the car. He just made a quick sketch so he could remember some of the important details he might want to write about. Then he wrote words and phrases that describe the car. Study Lee's observations.

top comes off

fins

red

shiny

Thunderbird

Grandpa

forty years old

looks like a rocket ship

whitewall tires

looks like new

lots of chrome

Your Own Observations

Draw a picture of your topic in the middle of this page. Then write descriptive words and phrases around it.

write

Using Senses to Describe

Your senses can help you describe. By including details from your senses in your writing, you can make your readers feel, smell, taste, hear, and see. Using your senses helps you create word pictures for your readers.

Lee used his senses to help describe his grandpa's car. He probably won't include all of these details in his essay, but he will use many of them. Let's take a look at his list. Notice how Lee used colorful and descriptive nouns, adjectives, verbs, and adverbs in his list.

Using My Senses to Describe

My topic is _Grandpa's T-bird_

I can see: cherry red paint
chrome so shiny that I can see my reflection
people smiling and pointing when they see the car go by

I can feel: smooth, cool metal
sharp fins in the back
soft seats

I can smell: gasoline
wax

I can taste: root beer floats, because Grandpa likes to get them
when we go out for drives

I can hear: purring engine
songs on the radio
wind whistling by

Think about your topic. In the space below, describe things about your topic that you can see, feel, smell, taste, and hear. Skip the ones that don't make sense for your topic. Which details will help you create a vivid word picture of your topic?

write

Using My Senses to Describe

My topic is _____

I can see:

I can feel:

I can smell:

I can taste:

I can hear:

Organizing Your Ideas

Your descriptive essay needs to have three parts:

✦ The **introduction** is the beginning of your essay. It will tell your readers what your topic is. It introduces your readers to your topic.

✦ The **body** is the middle of your essay. In this section, you will describe your favorite person, place, or thing.

✦ The **conclusion** is the end of your essay. In the conclusion, you will summarize your thoughts or tell how you feel about your topic. It lets your readers know that your essay is complete.

Lee decided to turn each part of his essay into a paragraph. He has organized his essay like this:

Paragraph 1: My introduction will tell *my readers that my essay will describe Grandpa's T-bird.*

Paragraph 2: The body of my essay will describe *some of the things I really like about the T-bird.*

Paragraph 3: My conclusion will tell *how I feel about Grandpa's T-bird.*

Your Organizing Plan

It's your turn to organize. Think about the ideas you want to include in your essay. Then use the space below to plan what you will say in each part of your essay.

write

Paragraph 1: My introduction will tell _____

_____

_____

_____

Paragraph 2: The body of my essay will describe_____

_____

_____

_____

Paragraph 3: My conclusion will tell _____

_____

_____

_____

discuss Share your paragraph ideas with your writing partner. Explain what you will write in each paragraph. Discuss these questions:

✦ Are your ideas organized in a logical order?

✦ What descriptive details will you include in each paragraph?

Drafting
Writing Your Rough Draft

Writing Good Paragraphs

During prewriting, you've identified many descriptive details about your topic. You've organized your ideas and decided what information you will put in each paragraph. Let's talk about paragraphs before you begin writing.

A **paragraph** is a group of sentences that relate to one idea. The first line of a paragraph is always indented.

✦ The **topic sentence** tells what the paragraph is about. It is usually the first sentence in the paragraph. The topic sentence should catch your readers' attention. It should make your readers want to read more.

✦ The **rest of the sentences** in the paragraph explain or describe the topic sentence. They provide details that support the topic sentence.

Read this paragraph from Lee's essay. The first sentence is the topic sentence. It tells you what he is going to write about in the paragraph. The rest of the sentences include the details.

Inside Grandpa's garage is the coolest car I've ever seen! It's a 1957 Ford Thunderbird. It is the first car he ever bought, and he has taken really good care of it. It looks like new, but it's over forty years old! He calls it the "T-bird."

Did Lee's topic sentence catch your attention? He hoped that it would make you want to find out more about the car. He hoped you would wonder what kind of car it is.

Your Rough Draft

Now you are ready to write your rough draft. This is your first chance to get all your ideas down on paper. The rough draft is the first version of your essay. Before you begin writing, take a look at these hints:

✦ Write to your **audience**. Before you begin, ask yourself, "**Who is going to read this essay?**" Describe your favorite person, place, or thing vividly for your audience so they can picture exactly what you are describing.

✦ Use the **organizing plan** that you wrote on page 17. Keep in mind what information you want to put in the **introduction,** the **body,** and the **conclusion** of your essay. Begin each paragraph with a good **topic sentence**.

✦ Use **colorful nouns, adjectives, verbs,** and **adverbs** in your essay. Include some of the **descriptive words and phrases** you wrote on pages 13 and 15.

A Title

Have you thought of a title for your essay? The title should

✦ **tell what your essay is about**

✦ **be short**

✦ **catch your readers' attention**

✦ **have all the important words capitalized**

write

Write your rough draft on a separate sheet of paper. If you write on every other line, your essay will be easier to read, revise, and edit. Don't worry about making mistakes—just write! You will be able to make changes and corrections later. Keep your rough draft in the front pocket of this book.

Revising
Making Revisions

When you revise, you rewrite parts of your essay to make it better. There are three words to remember when you revise:

✦ You **ADD** important information you have left out.

✦ You **DELETE** (get rid of) information you don't need.

✦ You **MOVE** information that is in the wrong place.

You also revise to make your words more interesting. Good writers choose words carefully. They try to use words that are colorful and exciting.

Writers use special editing symbols, or marks, to show how they want to change their work. You can see that Lee used some of these marks when he revised his essay. Take a look at the editing symbols on the back pocket of this book. You can use these marks when you revise and edit your essay.

Now look at the way Lee revised this paragraph from his essay. Study the changes. Can you see how they improve his writing?

I love Grandpa's T-bird, and so does he. The paint is cherry red. The T-bird looks like a small rocket ship with a round window
It has two doors and two bucket seats.
on each side. The front fenders stretch way out. The back fenders look like wings with little red lights. Grandpa calls them fins, but
and it's also a convertible
I think they look like jet engines. The T-bird has a hard top. But the top comes off! My neighbor has a convertible. One day, he forgot to put the top up, and it rained. His car was a mess.
The chrome is so shiny that I can see my reflection.

How Do You Know What to Revise?

Read your essay aloud. Listen as you read. Ask your writing partner to listen, too. You and your partner will probably hear some of the things that need to be changed.

◆ Listen for words that don't make sense.

◆ Listen for things that seem out of place.

◆ Ask yourself if you could add anything that might improve your description.

◆ Ask yourself if your readers will be able to picture exactly what you are describing.

discuss Discuss the changes that you think you should make with your writing partner. Listen to suggestions from your writing partner. Take notes to help you remember the changes you want to make.

write

Now it's time to revise your rough draft. Before you begin, read the revision checklist on the next page. Use the questions as a guide while you revise. Also, look at the editing symbols on the back pocket of this book. They will help you mark your changes.

Use a colored pen or pencil to mark your revisions. That makes them easy to see and read. Don't worry if your rough draft looks messy. Revising isn't always neat. Just be sure that you can understand what you have marked.

Remember these words: **ADD, DELETE,** and **MOVE**.

Checking Your Revisions

Check your revisions by answering the questions on this revision checklist. Then ask your writing partner to read your essay and answer the checklist questions, too.

Revision Checklist

| **Writer's Checklist:** | | | **Writing Partner's Checklist:** | |
Yes	No		Yes	No
☐	☐	Did I include an introduction, a body, and a conclusion?	☐	☐
☐	☐	Did I write a good topic sentence for each paragraph?	☐	☐
☐	☐	Did I include details that support each topic sentence?	☐	☐
☐	☐	Did I avoid repeating the same words over and over again?	☐	☐
☐	☐	Did I use my senses to describe my topic?	☐	☐
☐	☐	Did I use descriptive nouns, adjectives, verbs, and adverbs?	☐	☐
☐	☐	_____	☐	☐
☐	☐	_____	☐	☐

discuss Did you or your partner answer "No" to any of the questions? If so, discuss the problem. Ask your teacher for help if you are not sure how to correct the problem. Mark your corrections on your rough draft.

Is your rough draft getting all marked up and hard to read? That's okay. In fact, that's good! It shows that you have been thinking about your work.

Editing
Editing and Proofreading

Good writers edit their work to correct mistakes. They look closely at every word, every sentence, and every paragraph. Then they use the editing symbols to mark their mistakes.

Let's study the editing marks on Lee's essay. Can you see how the edits improve his writing?

¶ I hope Grandpa never gets rid of the T-bird. Sometimes we go for drives together. I like to feel the wind whisle (SP) through my hair. Grandpa likes root beer flotes (SP), so we often stop to get them. I like to lissen (SP) to the radio while we drive. Grandpa likes to lissen (SP) to the sound of the engine, he (RO) says it purrs like a Kitten. People often smile and wave when they see Grandpa drive the T-bird. Maybe someday I'll get to drive the T-bird, too!

write

It's your turn! Look at the proofreading checklist on the next page. Use the questions as a guide while you edit. Mark your edits with a colored pen or pencil. Remember to use the editing symbols on the back pocket.

Checking Your Edits

Check your edits by answering the questions on this proofreading checklist. Then ask your writing partner to read your essay and answer the checklist questions, too.

Proofreading Checklist

Writer's Checklist:			**Writing Partner's Checklist:**	
Yes	No		Yes	No
☐	☐	Did I spell all words correctly?	☐	☐
☐	☐	Did I indent the first line of every paragraph?	☐	☐
☐	☐	Did I capitalize the first word of every sentence?	☐	☐
☐	☐	Did I punctuate the end of each sentence correctly?	☐	☐
☐	☐	Did I avoid using run-on sentences?	☐	☐
☐	☐	Is my handwriting neat?	☐	☐
☐	☐	Is my title capitalized correctly?	☐	☐
☐	☐	_____	☐	☐
☐	☐	_____	☐	☐

discuss Did you or your partner answer "No" to any of the questions? If so, discuss the problem. Ask your teacher for help if you are not sure how to correct the problem. Mark all of your corrections on your rough draft.

Publishing Your Work

Lee has finished his essay. Let's take a look at it before you write your own essay.

Grandpa's T-bird

Inside Grandpa's garage is the coolest car I've ever seen! It's a 1957 Ford Thunderbird. It is the first car he ever bought, and he has taken really good care of it. It looks like new, but it's over forty years old! He calls it the "T-bird."

I love Grandpa's T-bird, and so does he. The paint is cherry red. The chrome is so shiny that I can see my reflection. The T-bird looks like a small rocket ship with a round window on each side. It has two doors and two bucket seats. The front fenders stretch way out. The back fenders look like wings with little red lights. Grandpa calls them fins, but I think they look like jet engines. The T-bird has a hard top, and it's also a convertible. The top comes off!

I hope Grandpa never gets rid of the T-bird. Sometimes we go for drives together. I like to feel the wind whistle through my hair. Grandpa likes root beer floats, so we often stop to get them. I like to listen to the radio while we drive. Grandpa likes to listen to the sound of the engine. He says it purrs like a kitten. People often smile and wave when they see Grandpa drive the T-bird. Maybe someday I'll get to drive the T-bird, too!

---

write

Now it's time for you to publish! Write your essay on the next two pages. As you write, remember to make all the changes you have marked.

Publishing Ideas

Writing is meant to be shared. You have just made a clean, neat copy of your work. Now you must decide two things:

✦ Who do you want to read your work?

✦ How should your work be shared?

Here are some ideas from Lee and his classmates. Read them. Then add your own ideas to the list.

write

Ideas for Publishing a Descriptive Essay

1. Make drawings of the people, places, and things you and your classmates chose to describe.

2. Share your descriptive essays with another class and ask them to draw a picture of each description.

3. Collect copies of all of the essays your class wrote. Make a book called Our Favorite People, Places, and Things.

_____

_____

_____

write

Think about the different ways that you can publish your work. Then write an answer to the following question:

How will you share your work?

I will share my work by _____

_____

Prompts for Future Writing

You as a Writer

You are a writer! You've worked through the writing process. You've written a descriptive essay. The more you practice, the better writer you will be. So let's think about what you can write in the future.

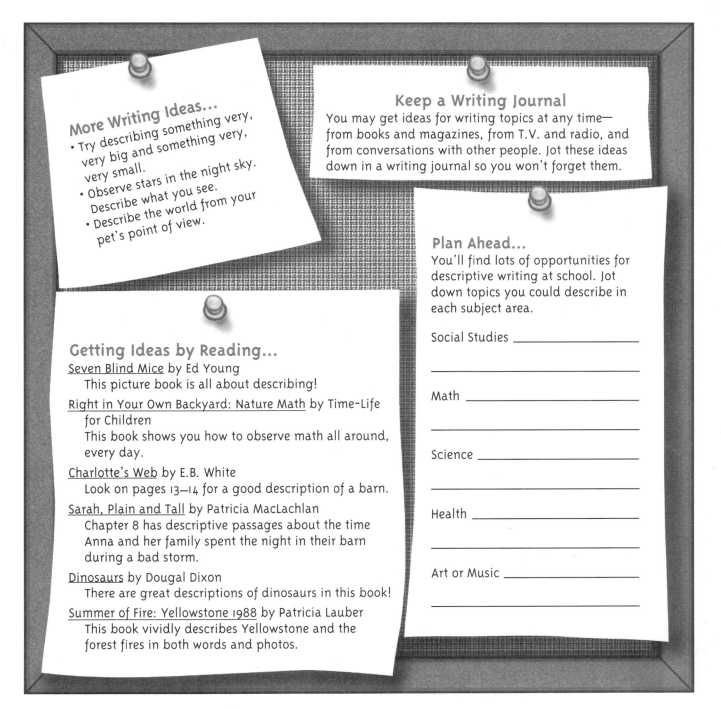

More Writing Ideas...
- Try describing something very, very big and something very, very small.
- Observe stars in the night sky. Describe what you see.
- Describe the world from your pet's point of view.

Keep a Writing Journal
You may get ideas for writing topics at any time—from books and magazines, from T.V. and radio, and from conversations with other people. Jot these ideas down in a writing journal so you won't forget them.

Plan Ahead...
You'll find lots of opportunities for descriptive writing at school. Jot down topics you could describe in each subject area.

Social Studies _____

_____

Math _____

_____

Science _____

_____

Health _____

_____

Art or Music _____

_____

Getting Ideas by Reading...
<u>Seven Blind Mice</u> by Ed Young
    This picture book is all about describing!
<u>Right in Your Own Backyard: Nature Math</u> by Time-Life for Children
    This book shows you how to observe math all around, every day.
<u>Charlotte's Web</u> by E.B. White
    Look on pages 13–14 for a good description of a barn.
<u>Sarah, Plain and Tall</u> by Patricia MacLachlan
    Chapter 8 has descriptive passages about the time Anna and her family spent the night in their barn during a bad storm.
<u>Dinosaurs</u> by Dougal Dixon
    There are great descriptions of dinosaurs in this book!
<u>Summer of Fire: Yellowstone 1988</u> by Patricia Lauber
    This book vividly describes Yellowstone and the forest fires in both words and photos.

Timed Writing

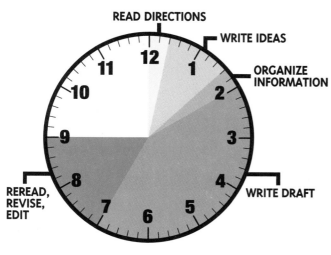

45 minutes

Have you ever taken a timed writing test? Did it make you nervous? Were you afraid that you might not be able to finish?

The key to successful timed writing is **PLANNING**. You need to figure out how to spend your time. Let's pretend that you have been given 45 minutes to write an essay. This is what you would need to do:

1. **Read and think about the DIRECTIONS.** Be sure that you understand exactly what you are supposed to do.
(Suggested time: 2 minutes)

2. **Write down your IDEAS for the assignment.** What do you want to say? What are your main ideas? What details will you include?
(Suggested time: 6 minutes)

3. **ORGANIZE your information.** Remember that you will need an introduction, a body, and a conclusion.
(Suggested time: 2 minutes)

4. **WRITE a draft.** Take your time here. Think as you write. Follow your plan.
(Suggested time: 25 minutes)

5. **REREAD, REVISE, and EDIT your work.**
(Suggested time: 10 minutes)

Portfolio Assessment Sheet

Congratulations! You've learned the steps in the writing process. You've finished your essay.

This page will help you think about what you have learned. The next page will help you find out what other people think about your writing. You can use this assessment sheet to evaluate everything you write this school year.

_____Evaluating Your Work_____

First, let's review. List the steps in the writing process.

1. _____

2. _____

3. _____

4. _____

5. _____

What did you enjoy the most? _____

_____

_____

_____

Which part of the writing process was hardest for you?_____

_____

_____

_____

What other topics would you like to write about? _____

_____

_____

_____

Let's find out what other people think about your work. Sharing your work is a good way to get opinions, good advice, and maybe even a few compliments!

Ask your teacher, a classmate, and another adult to write a brief evaluation of your work in the space below.

Learning From Others

Name of teacher: _____

Comments: _____

_____

_____

_____

_____

Name of classmate: _____

Comments: _____

_____

_____

_____

_____

Name of other adult: _____

Comments: _____

_____

_____

_____

_____